MW01205474

HERE on Earth
· · · · · · · · ·

HERE
on Earth

59 sonnets

Larry Goodell

La Alameda Press *Albuquerque*

The author is grateful for the previous publication of ::
Garden (*La Alameda Press* broadside); Ode to Lenore (*Puerto del So; Conjunctions*);
Compost (*Albuquerque Living*); Free Spirit (*Puerto del Sol*);
And Eight Thousand Stars (*Huevos*); Gemini in the Forest (*Sulphur*);
Art With a Capital T (*Fishdrum*); New Mexico Style (*Sulphur*);
and The House That Makes It So (*New Mexico Poetry Renaissance,* Red Crane Press).

ISBN :: I-888809-00-0
Library of Congress Number :: 96-84329

Cover photograph © :: Lenore Goodell
Frontispiece photograph © :: Cirrelda Snider-Bryan

•

La Alameda Press
9636 Guadalupe Trail NW
Albuquerque, New Mexico 87114

for Lenore
&
Joel

Contents

$\mathcal{T}$o the right, honorable, dignified, most
holy, aloof, superior interior exterior being,
gentleman & lady, above in the 13th heaven looking down on
our species' follies, may you prosper in limitless longevity,
flowers of all the fruit trees of spring to you in bountiful tulip to
daffodil, grape hyacinth to sour cherry, post-equinoctial burst of renewed
gladness and glee, I your fateful servant most humble human poet offer
these play-songs, these little real surprises, as spring trinkets to you
that when strung together may garland you with everything I have
to blossom together this sequence this necklace of little sounds, odes,
melodies, sonnets to you, these song nets catch my life devotion to you
Meso America All
America
Grandma-Grandpa
Ometéotl
Mother & Father of all of us
sprung up from the earth
I offer these in sunlight, the moonlight our own light
oh
Thank you humbly
I do with this gift.

Your listening servant,
Larry Goodell
Placitas, New Mexico

Centerpiece

I came to wear my buttons.
But a psychologist said that would be worshipping Freud.
Now Jung said he was a very old man.
A fraud, actually.
They got into a fight & knocked me down.
I'm a center for Angels.
Life is a screw, a nail said to me.
A hammer replied, it's all in your head.
Sing, you with wings, & button your coat
The more I write, the younger I get.
The more I paint, the older I get.
The more I create artificial fruit,
the wealthier I get.
That's why I'm so heavy, and wear a light suit.

Garden

You are the apple of my egg
the leg of anything of God gave
to Queen, to Goddess, Right
you are, left, woman, apple,
Chicken, Rooster, Comb, Turkey,
Roof, low line of adobes meet
jagged, hot out of the blue, the sun
moon's cold face, the Poles
Kissing hot center, water
        carries pails of meaning up
the hill to fall, Jack failed
not to hit, Jill assumed
the crown Jewels in rice, thrown
birdseed instead, the hummingbirds after
        everything red in
the garden of even.

Air

May the this of the that be those
the tip of the hat be toes—
may the whorled infancy of broccoli
& the denied spaghetti go back to Italy.
May Isaac Stern go back to France
and Franco Beltrametti come to prance the Swiss franc
up the Alps of America, once again before I die
may a horseopera kiss a fly and every—
thing, every jerk, every comeuppance baboon
be the tragic relief of academic comedy
closely exchanged trains & uplifted pantaloons
excuse me, silk bikinis or 19*th* Century tub wear
Come out to the conservatory dear, and out of the hat,
out of the hat, let's pull some air.

Home Cave

Writing is the most successful telling of yourself to Courage—
Queen of the Lion Heart, the Grizzly Bear Attacker
Strength bending down to touch you, touch me, show
Herself out of the Tarot, out of the cage, out of the Forest
the Jungle Subconscious, the Unconscious deep as the cave of the
Earth
where we shake grizzly hands and come out of the swamp to set
the forests burning
Burning burning bright as we stay up fighting all night
and go to bed at dawn friends, learning how to fight again
learning how to write again, learning how to walk again
learning how to lose hair, losing hair under the Crown
as each takes her turn, Queen-King for a Day, well
it's learning ABC's and exhilerating art of breathing
while you breathe, and breathing while you meet your maker
who's your wife and husband, reading writing late at night.

Suicide

"I am comfortably numb." Oh Blessed oblivion
I want out. Suicide has been on the increase since
Marilyn Monroe died. This phenomenon of cluster suicide
is growing like everything like mold like flies
like the lies of summer, I mean, specifically, put under glass
the pizza parlor drug case, the insistence of calling a rubber
a condom, the enlarging of the test of the bomb
I mean blowing it up at the factory to see if it works—
you blow it up as big as a watermelon then
you know no babies will be hatched. Everybody
is scared of society & Society is scared
of everybody. Springtime is the most beautiful,
when non-blowing, season, I mean the winds haven't
discovered us yet and I want to go on living.

After the Sun

Wait wait wait, until tomorrow morning
Until you have the light of day from the dawn.
Everything is different after Earth's turning
And the miseries have gone down all night long.
That's where everything begins for everybody
As the light passes inch by inch along the globe
And sooner or later you wonder if there's another
Life or habitat anything like our World Home.
Nothing spares me, thoughts and actions, vacancies of intellect
Swirls of bodies fill and empty
As I spread manure and turn the tilth the worm's exposed tracks
The wind, the cold, the fake Winter lays the last blame.
   I rush in to cook, an Indian feast and let
   The day fall away long after raging sun's set.

March 19*th*

The swallows came back to Capistrano this year as they do
every year on the Feast of St. Joseph's as Laguna Pueblo
dances, and the hymn to her to Spring begins, I saw you breaking
ground, we sat around then stood up crashing
our heads through the ceilings and the worms ate in
and out and didn't harm us as we ate their castings
up the holy moment of the isolated shell of singing in
the words delivering blue scilla, purple iris reticulata
meticulous beginners—crocus, winter aconite blinking out as
the yellow species tulips & the red their heads close to ground
close in evening, opening morning, tulips rippling pointed
up, daffodils blading up, we are the I-am-it-they-are
I'm going out of the prison winter's last leg, I broke my
shell, I'm just a spring chicken, a March 19*th* day given.

Ode to Lenore

Ode to Steve in the form of a sonnet, a lyric poem
of 14 lines, a line laid down like a row of bricks
or rather bricks (adobe) laid down in the rising
wall the dream of building row by row com-
radery and fun and go, ode to the other Steve and then
no ode, a sad expanse of only me, myself and
I, just living deliciously in spite of commentaries,
introductions and lit crit seductions, oh cutter
of awful, sliding through the air to root in spring
sink down the hindsight, simply be, an ode to
odometers, oh no, squeaking doors, oh no, cat shit, oh
no, an ode to birthdays, a mood swing that jazzes out on
even keel, a verging love, I swear I'm a Quaker animist
misting orchids, ferns & cacti, an Ode to Lenore until I die.

Ode to Song

The most wonderful imaginable things happen to you when you're
Blessed by the onus, the curse, the habit of being a poet—
Once you're marked, it is a birthmark, an aging, blurring
Tattoo you wish you'd never had but know, no!
You can't say that, the most wonderful powers
And contentments come to you when you're blessed by all
This awful talent, word jazz, link to the Blue Sky
Through this Goddamn God Band, this personal, non-public
Universality, the exalted ego on stilts brought down to
The mere Human Being, how appreciative the stereotyping
Poetry pigeon-holing audience that shoved your life-thing
Under the rug since high-school and in thanks and hearing
Turns deaf ears to your inflated past, present, future
How dare you find life with meaning & an unadulterated song
                                        surprise?

Strawberries

Out of it is in and up and picking
up against the wind that measures spring
and entering cold with a fist around the hoe
and leveling what was a hill into an irrigated flow
that curves in waves that hold the water
as against uncommon cold I spread manure
and peat moss and rototill it in & rake
and set in bone meal & cottonseed meal
for these Scott Strawberries to spread their roots
through as I set them against the wavy bank
their pruned roots out flat, shallow feeders
with scrub oak leaf mulch topping, dirt
over them & water long and deep at last after the last
winter blast late in March I hope these babies find a home.

A Magic

Magic is the formative power of thingamajig humble jumble
ride on the magic carpet till the light bulb surprise Aladdin's lamp
ghosts chance out of a hat, open sesame, "a garden by the water"
becomes faith, grace, & reality, a straw saving a life
removed from the camel's back, something in another room
come into this one with light and illusion, the fact sexualized,
lionized, idealized, rhapsodic, defined, woven in and out of self
Maya pigeonholed, the wish truthed, the self betrothed
the famous ancient Eastern light, the day created
out of day, enchanted night created out of night.
A man is a donkey, a donkey a man, a
woman a spider, a spider a shark, a monkey
an astronaut, out of nowhere I mean a floating garden
I mean the surprise of everything intended swept away new.

A Writer's Life

for Dagoberto Gilb

Why write? Fame, shows, flowers, mental
stability, flattery, corruption, shame, glee
it's pleasing, credits, feathers, fine hats, insults
the stability of infinity, the future of posterity, the
recurring theme of a classic, the one and only, reflection,
conception with God, odes, conniptions, ribbons,
dejections, miseries, happiness for moments, suicides
stabilities, eternities, other worlds, the right heres,
political invective, love, love, love in bed again
family, children, if any, if any, the tilt of
the imagination, creative uplift, there's plenty
of bathrooms, wars, treaties, nature, home
back to the movement movement, it's everything
that you can manage, anything you can imagine if
you have the music, it'll sweep you away for life, life.

Spring Fancy

Green Chile is the Jack of Diamonds, Red Chile
The hors d'oeuvre express, the foundation cream
Anaheim the Go-between, Pasilla the Rock-Hard
Generic, Jalapeño the Red White & Blue, Ancho the
Beautyrest Mattress, Bell Pepper the Paris suburb
Cayenne the ball park, Peter Pepper the Shrunken Head
Aha! a Surprise! Meaning! Life has a moment of
Passing fancy! Need! Argument! Logic! Words
that hold Water! Water that holds the bucket upside-
down, the floating bucket the clouds, the clouds holding
up the sky that's here   the Volcanic mesas hold
the sky to the Earth   Slope the Earth to the River
slopes up the incline   landscape of juniper and
arroyos   to the worked land just out of
my window, the light pulls ready for the first plants.

On Too Long

To the trees, the breeze, the bees, within the seven seas
the ease with which I eat my cheese
the nuclear freeze, the teas of the English
the tragic disease that cheats you, fleas—
knees, seize the tonic of the moment, Keats
Nietzsche, Matisse, geese & fields
of eats, the heat, a neat seat, the elite
the wrong, the gong, the too long song
the gallumphing along to please the ear, tongs
on the dawn, pulling mind-boggling togs
off Gods Goddesses, holy harem knocks the bong
over, gasps smoke, the throng talks, louder
glowing & throwing, gloating, we got you
going, got you rocking, a naked tease, the trees,
the glee, the wrong, a loosened thong.

Necktie

(hold tie up, pulling neck)

Pontificate, beguile, and sweat, organize, spray with,
faction out, decentralize, circumcise, pull the wool over,
standardize, beef up, swirl, marble, whirl,
chatter, asphyxiate, sue, night light, stand up to,
drive up, moralize, go to church, fear, hate
not quite elate, fix, charge in, order
puncture, tire, sour, fish, shoot,
catch, deepen, fry, bulldoze, arrange
categorize, go after, fence, blow up
be taken care of, murder, circumvent
tower, cheapen, gird, engineer, bet
seduce, reduce, destroy, love, duck
manipulate, fire, fuck, give up, shit
die, kiss, charge, avoid, beat it, buy.

Nah!

I'm an organicist no, a romanticist no,
a futurist no, a simpletonian no, a surrealist
no, a post-industrialist no, a computer writer chip
no, a fuzzy thinker no, an objectivist no,
a projectivist. No, a decentralist. No, a freelance
populist. No, a frustrated entertainer. No,
a poet-singer. No, a scratchy story-teller. No,
a nervous ding batter. No, a pseudo-academic.
No, a mini-entrepreneur. No, a part-time performer.
No, a weekend competitor. No, just more creative baggage.
No, a buzzline out of focus. No, a socio-satiricist. No,
a scatological realist. No, a lover of word tunes.
No, a pagan out of place. No, a wind follower. No,
an electronic music toy operator. Nah, a design-buffoon.

Quote the Breath

Do sudden shifts in the rain foretell a bad summer?
When the rain falls at a 90° angle to where it has fallen?
And then goes up back toward the clouds then turns back
down fountaining on itself it drops in splashes
having gone in square circles? What a curiosity
weather-watching is. Who looks out the window to predict
what's going to happen? A female grosbeak has arrived
black-spotted white & a brown blur, red, red eyes.

Is nature fact or fiction? Don't some categories hold?
Isn't something precious if it reveals to you a sudden
instant thing—a surprise of applause that is the gut
response to something light and unimaginable?
That came like an unheard song that was more than real
and made you feel good, good, good? Quote the breath?

Compost

So let us forget foul songs and bad breath—
imagined wrongs and stabs in the back
the jockeying to win to win to win as
competition robs you of friendship, friendship—
that it's a gift pouring out, pouring out,
whether taken or even seen by anyone, let's
forget we don't forgive, forgive each other
we don't forget—that somehow the burning issue
is the trash, the bridges, the flies, the cold shoulders
the rotten tomatoes and potatoes, you take it all
to the dump, "sanitary landfill" they say,
whatever you say, we can be friends again,
that knits together again over lost time, that old shirt,
that old skirt, that old hurt, that compost, that trash, that dirt.

A Definition

I live for definition. And that's where going crazy slowly
makes sense to me. I can't help the delineation of the body
or who it defines, as carefully as words. I can't help myself.
I lack controls. I am that lack. I simply know
that definition isn't academic. I'm with the mob,
the mob as carefully defined at I. As me. As you.
As "As" is—rounded and pointed & tipped & flowing.
The power that came from chasing animals for food,
I guess, & later, farming. I garden, the muscles move
the hoe that moves the earth around. The bending
bulges, the writing, defines, the character of power
is in the riding of the flesh, the contours, the forms,
the architecture of meaning. Back to physical beauty
that comes & goes as naturally as I know this is built &
                                    so casually defined.

"I"

Yesterday my ears dropped off, the day before my thumbs
A week ago my toes dropped off, and now goes my gums
My heart fell out, my eyes and nose, and now my belly button
My butt fell off and then my knees followed by kidneys
What a state I'm in I can't run or do anything
But think the thoughts I'm given, but then half of my
Brain dropped off and now I'm truly driven
One lung, now two I cannot breathe & now my stomach falls
All my entrails fall out, my legs, my arms, my balls,
My hair my skull, my trunk, my cock, my God
I've lost my rocks, my marbles, my soul drops out
My spirit, my energy, my entropy, my will, my urge
My life, my dreams, my memories, my responsibilities
My ego, my everything, my my, my me, my I.

The Face of God

If both numbers on the telethon match the size of his eyeballs
you have won 100,000 dollar instant winner chance to be
the one to be the one to be the one to be *the* one to be
the order of the century your half-price magazines, your bloated
dishes, half-diamonds, sensate lingerie, rose hedges,
miracle bath water with crucifix shower head, send in your
order by May *1st*, affix the gold seal instant Cadillac hearse
bonus prize stamp to your order of every magazine
of the universe including sub-machine guns, automatic bazookas
and power shot hefty car opener screaming security
crook-hooks and 10 million dollars will be added to
your bonus 100,000 every week for life
by watching telethon give-away of God's eternal paste-up church
tear-off this portion with your magic instant numbers, watch the
                                        size of
                        his eyes.

Piece of Dust

I can't do anything because the death of sky is abrupt
and the well-known forces below suck.
Whether to change into them and become a turncoat is moot
But not for me, I don't exist I'm not even a toot-toot,
A flute, a piccolo, a fife, a wife to fortune, a husband
to anything, which is the story of the ego, the popped balloon
is not the ego, the great big "I" that not even death could kill.
I came back to life having never died and I don't think I'm
better than anyone else, I'm just all I know and
those killers, those greedy bastards, those with nothing
in their veins but blood, with nothing in their hearts
but a heart, nothing in their heads but a fish, might be
beneath me as unknown winking tiny star, piece of dust
against the light, cool night lessens the sight of all that's me.

Oh No

(syrupy voice)

Design your flowers with nature in mind
your people with a conservative bent
make your cats & dogs cooperative
your freeways with just the right curves in them
your robots well oiled & with quiet circuitry
make your landscapes pleasing to the eye—
eliminate weeds, nor let the buildings grow too tall
make all your poets self-employed versifiers
your carpenters & map-makers busy as bees
design those TV's with remote controls and
eliminate violence from them, and let there be
no sibling rivalry or economic problems
so nations can lie down at peace with each other and
your mellow planet will not be rotten to the core oh
                                        no, oh no.

Art with a Capital T

for Robert Winson

Ode to the ode ode odor, Berg-Webern hors d'oeuvres
Frill stuck to the walls and eaten off lick by lick
Until the 19*th* C. turned into *1905* and the smell
Of War tore art off the walls, onto the floor
Out the back alley, to the dump, nothing was left
But the four walls of a bare gallery, a couple hi-fi speakers
An AR turntable, Berg's string quartet or rather
Webern's or Schoenberg's, the time is *1935.*
Everything has been heard before, no frills, only the thrill
Of Vestige avant-garde, the ultimate up direction
Of music, the first movement precedes the *2nd* but not
The fourth, everything reverses, cubistically or
Dodecaphonically, the extreme instance of the intense
The pure here-after, the "now" on a high Duchamp stool,
                                        A-r-r-T!

New Mexico Style

Oh Sky that is my bosom, Flower that is my defect,
How the Southwest lifts me to enchantment,
Enchantment of moron over dolt, enrapture of the mesa
Catty-corner across from McDonald's in Bernalillo.
My high-flying boots straddle that bohemian cactus there
And it's pleasure! Only a woman would know.
My river goddess Alpha Romero speeds down the Interstate:
These stones are my inner tones, and Nature marches on.
Coyote is a woman, woman is a muchacha grown up to señora,
The sky is full of rainbows over the Chile Harbor
Where the Rio Grande meets the infinite, the infinite turquoise
                                                    drama.
My grandmother showed me everything I know back in Brooklyn
"Come to New Mexico, they'll love you there—there're
More of us there than the natives, and we populate and shit in
                                                    style."

A Cookbook

We've got our peopled onions & cloves stuck in a vibration booth:
good cooking is how to make swans or
sticking to a theme is only human if you don't want
to fly off the planet, which gravity, brother to sanity,
protects. Something can always be gleaned from
a poem about cooking, as everything builds in
the machine of learning which computerized disks only
imitate, it's back to tired counsel about the family, or
a gap in the conversation in which love and
a certain learned familiarity are all that matters.
He was seen on TV eating spaghetti after,
of course, they showed how to prepare it and
he was her cousin, though not by blood, they knew
so much in common we ate everything they brot from the kitchen.

The Library of Knowhow

Lawnmower of forgetful feet, mow my grass—
No, more than grass, my consciousness—Intercepted
Transmogrified, Photosynthesized, Hybridized
Eternalized in Nothing, Clippings, mere Clippings.
I am the Compost of Futurity, Don't give me up:
Better yet, give all of me up. Will I give myself up?
I get mowed down, lost is the least desire,
A psychic vacuum pulverized by reality,
Every bit & piece of it, every day, as anybody knows.
Or as I, now a nobody knows. Nobody knows.
Goodbye experts and advanced degrees, power on platforms
Ivory Towers of the necessary "There"—the Library of Knowhow
Somehow turned over to the public which I have become—
In honest, day to day, hard rock, how-to-do-it facts.

Free Spirit

for Lee Connor

Everything is in archetypal leaps.
What is what you're saying if it's not interesting?
You were the avant-garde podner.
Your hayloft is your head, your halo your lariat.
You are an entirely new Virgin & Mary.
You are the baby of heterodoxus.
Your shape is always different from what your parents was.
You drink kilos. You eat thousands of foods.
Everything you say forms a letter of delight.
You are not Christian, Buddhist or Hindu
You are Joseph or Jonathan.
You are a Free Spirit—you have no fire you have no water
Until you are born again into yourself
You are the earth floating with wit, with everything you are.

Too True

I don't have the iron clad genes of genius,
I have the origins of talent. Where second-best
is the cake you eat most. You don't apologize
for the candles, you give them the hole in the ghost.
And they give you Pagan Woman, the Hostess
with the Most.
                      She becomes pregnantly Earth Woman
and Wonder Woman Wishes *au contraire.*
The talent I have given you is red white & blue—
my costume super wonder woman amplified in blue,
becomes green takes on changing everywhere it goes.
Where it goes no mighty knows, but your talent is blessed.
The Earth comes up saying it, the answer, answer last—
    When was the last time you had a blast?
    Why is it Age tends to make it all too true?

The Performance

for Nathaniel Tarn & Janet Rodney

Language should do something other than pray for reality to
                      come true.
Poetry should be assessed by millions like real estate.
Exclusivity is the paranoia of the ivory tower.
When you pull words out of a skull's eyes they take on more
                      meaning.
To perform something dead is a valued ridding of the carcass.
You start with stimulation and proceed to the utmost banality.
Everything is stress & regress, a dream of something funny,
                      a story in reverse.
Don't divulge when you stop, but stop with a bang.
If surprise is anything then imagination will destroy it.
The freedom to create is the passion of the wealthy.
A truly created thing is a joy for the creator.
Performed right with style adds wit to nonsense.
Bring everything out that the dim birds overlooked.
Punctuality is second to dependability, but be there in live
                      costume.

Returning

I live in my small self, breaking mists into clouds,
Removing the skull so the brain can travel
That far piece, that rocky place, where a trail
Changes into five or six colors and you wish
You were a geologist, the red in the rocks stands out
Against the blue of the wind in the sky, as everything
Spins out below you. I was on Peyote Rock
That *was* Cocktail Rock and now I'm sure is
A perch for viewing again perhaps a
Meditation point, I don't know what that is—
I've always traveled in myself, and there with
The Jemez capped by Redondo, the weaving of
The Rio Grande pulls the green all together in
A dry state, the space is always moving.

Magic Stone

To make something lively as a setting stone
The kind you meet in a fairy tale, around the bend
And suddenly you're in and all the leaves haven't dropped off
The trees, the trees—oh forest glen an' evergreens
The kind you end up teething on, Ponderosa Pine needles
To wash your dishes, and the praying, setting stone is really
Buzzing and alive with insect life: You drop the rock
Afraid you will get bit. And it floats, oval, insects of
All-life-Earth-knows in on it, as it heats glows that salmon-
Pink orange-red, shrinks or rather drops back, down
A tremendous heat out of sight to the Earth's core.
And this dirt and whip of ocean covering life in miniature
Steams up from it in a throbbing globe, pierced, crazed
Wholed, raised, loosened out in every single sight.

And Eight Thousand Stars

And eight thousand monomaniacal stars were exploded out
And that was the daddy, the ditty, that did it.
The soul scraped back against the dirt, the resistance
Between her & him, the backfire from the muffler
8000 particles out of the exhaust pipe, stars in trained explosion
Trained by eye and energy, everything out from center
From nothing between the resistance, the hand clap, pop of eye
Out & up from evacuating tube, a natural thrust pop
All things are natural in these times, of time before the time
Up and out of the cave, the long skinny cave, throbbed in
Painted walls in, carved in, up out of in exploding stars
That is sparks, wall of volcanos in the fuck vision of first time
Cummed out, caved in, strung bolted out, to be on the way
To become, fire, galactic spastic spaced out on call to life lives.

Honest, Oh Boy

for Bob Creeley

Again it is hitting the words free
Out of the block of imploded misuse
Mr. Singer You, time to see you again
When there isn't any time 2000 miles apart,
To hear, the architecture of your presence
Is an old friend and a glimpse of when
We were around the kitchen table far into the night.
When they were out to get some fresh air
And there was the moon out there and the light
Over the table stark high energy that in there
Was you, I was just a seed boy at heart
Unrealized I would devote my life to plants
And performance of the slings of words at
My heart, literally, through your guidelines honest.

One One

Oh young one one, he was smiling as only
A buddy out of the blue can, you wanted to see
You see, to bring me the Stroh's, to sweep
The floor of the pizza Parlor, to wear
An apron, a moustache, a duck-bill hat, advertising
Me, me, me, everything in the parlor is me, I mean
I'm here, this is all me as I face out into him
He wants to go outside where it's beautiful—
The sun, the pre-spring warmth, the attraction
Of male to male in outings, the baseball season
Soon, the garden pulling, the bed, my wife.
The energies of someone being simply genuinely
Nice—without frills—honest connection of Strangers
Renews, the hope, digs the ditches of Spring.

Song Word First

for Drummond Hadley

Without the flair there is no dare, no care
to go up all the way from the seed, the given
the base-foundation-grounding everything is *that*—
the sperm out of the blue the egg out of the green
the orange cap burst back, the skull cap
of plant of animal, buzz, ball, socket, fine
moire spiral DNA staircase up the mystery
murdered death, the covers laid back, the filament
the filum, brushed aside, the earth spurts, the waves
of "channelled" muses, gods, vibrations, harmonies
discordant atmospheres, electric brain charged
to zap it out, the arc, the pop the age-old song
the birth rock-daddy, seashell woman, be still ha ha!
everything else is enhancement of this song word first.

Orion

Orion, bastion of subcultures, holder
Of infamy in the best sense, progenitor of change—
Oh underground, underdog, sub-carpet, dive
Where the *free* reign, Kings & Queens of the Future,
Telling Fantastic stories under the stars under the ceilings—
In the weavings of dance which is closest to the heart,
Previous to the flamboyant avant-garde, the air
Before the steps of the army of culture, oh
Beneficial bacteria, lead us in art in the art of life
Oh stars of what's left of constellations
Still be our myth, my guiding light, sights
My visitation through the rainbow in the caves of secret meetings—
Orion, my favorite bold conspirator, conquistador
Of change, soft part below your belt shines down.

Reincarnation

"Art is nothing more than the electrocution of humanity,"
The spark of the dandy, in honest people's working worlds,
A patch to hang up, something told about to stare
But not too long, something above the furniture,
A sofa pleaser, something worth something—
Does the gallery keep you informed of the artist's worth?
But in my daily dreams, something rivets the fascination
Onto the spine onto the wall, into the act of dance
Where the created bustling bounces in the ears—
Lives were drawn & quartered to get to sophistication
Early lines crossed, zapped out caves, paintings
Chants for food, the Earth turning to the sun,
The brain wave picked up everything known with
Magnetism, death to life in instant pleasure.

Song It

for Steve Sullivan

The edge of the paper is it and if you're tidy
You won't spill over in the margins and it
Will often be about 5 beats per line or
The song of 4 will reassert itself from youth
And the Power Culture of America without the K.
Oh pop, oh obscure, oh him, himself, Mr. Beautiful
Overlaying the Dark Lady of the Sonnets as
She rises up from Gaia and Earth Spirits crave
something with structure, oh anything will do
When doodling is dead, your past is ahead.
The young man who asked for my ID, the "flatterer"
Brought me my beer, and all is energy when
You're most going, I swear by my Gods & Goddesses
And they swear by me: to stop on time is sublime.

Post-Modern Sex

Oh Macho Man, be my Clitoris Hippy,
Stars caterwaul and tongues depress
"I'm gone, I'm gone," she said entering Gertrude Stein.
He was too tough to be worth anything & the world,
heated up, worshiped him. As everything got tougher,
She declined, and then Gertrude Grob-Prandel, Wagnerian
Soprano, overfat but aware, and then, and then
Gertrude Lawrence. Lawrence, St. Laurence, St. Gertrude.
Oh rivers of the mind, repressed Earth—the cat's
In heat, the greenhouse is in heat, the vibrant tie-die shirts
And splattered painter's pants: everything's
Screaming for seduction but afraid, and thus
A book gets read, a writing written, a positivist structuralist
Theory posed, a rule stretched to its limits, and broken into
                                        orgasm.

Education of a Sonnet

A Sonnet, semiotics of phonics, the master begetter of
The master begetter, the mistress-master, the sign
Of signs, where everything learned as a child is in neon.
Your name in neon you learn it, your learning visualized
You name it, play games with it, it takes over
As you age, I age in names, I sound till found
And round the corner of squares in ivory, towering
Prolifically, scale to everyday heights as
Theory throbs to its last murdering self, and its
monetary clique hangs on into culthood, making
money out of plastics, as quality floors manhood
and soaring becomes flight of heart, heart
an organ transcended, the body saw thru soul
as the magician is an elementary teacher, Miss Brown, Miss Smith,
Miss Woo.

Spring Child

for Michael & Judy

Oh Birth, that is the Thirst, that changes everything
Thank God for the Telephone, the Freedom to Ring.
Oh Children of our lives, and ongoing Telegram
I morse-code you, somehow synchronicity works
When it works—I call David & he says
Michael & Judy had her baby Emily today,
And we wonder getting older if it's worth it not
To let our defenses down to say something simple:
How opposite to machinations of the intellect, Birth.
Or robots turning out ever more computer gizmos
As everything pops up around us in Spring—
I always want to drink water, & beer, milk—
The breast, the sky, the rain, this Spring, this April,
This Emily, this birth, this cherry, daffodil tulip apple bee
                                        blossom time.

Hard Wind Spring

Who knows what gives the Godawful breeze its suspenders
That can be yanked out of Hell so easily
Held up from Hell on the Face of the Earth
                    Is there any doubt Hell doesn't exist?
With Visions tearing up the Trees at Night
Visions of Apples and Pears and Pomegranates
Being attacked by gentle Punkers,
                    their Wild, Inflamed Hair
and Mohawk Tattoos lighting up the Dark.
                              Winds from Baby Breezes
Pretend to be tough.
                    These Southwest Mesas
Or are they Northeast Dive Bombers
        Are ruined by the Winds of Spring, the Pretensions
That anything exists. "Purity Sucks" said the Devil
Who's a figment of Prunehood,
                              and it's all
Storytelling, with a Heart of Mold, or Spring itself may
                              blow away.

In Performance of the Question

I must connect with someone who loves the language in
Vachel Lindsay, Abraham Lincoln, Otto Jesperson,
The OED, Allen Ginsberg, Dylan Thomas, Gertrude Stein,
                                                                          of course,
Ed Sanders, Sonia Sanchez, Lenore Kandel, Joanne Kyger,
Louise Beebe Wilder, Janet Cannon, Drummond Hadley,
Adlai Stevenson, Miriam Sagan, John Wieners, Robert
Duncan, Charles Olson picking up fragments of paper and
reading, aloud, why isn't there a word, between that &
performing, why is it so embarrassing not to make your wave
in print, but in local voice, I mean, it is, extended
like the family tree in a fan shape, *not* a pyramid
up, I say, read aloud, not recite but I guess, *perform*
Shit! from the page, the ages of music correspond, this is
a sonnet of the love between the voice & the page.

Is

"Today is the tomorrow you worried about yesterday"
but tomorrow is the sorrow that flowers aren't around
even the birds, even the air, the water, humankind.
Or tomorrow is simply today in a cycle that never ends.
We're all on coils asleep, awake, eating—forgetting—
Around and ahead or is it behind, I wish the coil was
Around and behind, tomorrow becomes yesterday:
that is the Romantic in me, how gorgeous the Dark Ages,
Now that seems defeatist even if they were illuminated,
And the music both in and out the Church was bouncy.
I guess I'd rather go forward picking up the backward as I go,
If I go anyplace with absence of power-money
Only me, a family, a house, and gardens, some friends
determined, where yesterday always becomes today, today.

Gemini in the Forest

"Language is spoken sound" as we mish-mash together
In the deep dark pandering forest we are on the crotch of the
                                                            whore
Nature is the prince, the princess king, the Queen the precise
                                                            bitch
The everything we adore—my alter-ego and I, my other self
My imagining traveling partner, my itching companion
The Dante Troubadours are singing in the kitchen, kitchen of
                                                            the forest
I am discovering myself here interfering in all art
That comes my way, the devouring of everything in its path
The packing away every crumb in ant caverns below
The eating away of every log from the heart within
The misadventure of hope and absurdity of human depression:
I'm just in the way—unless I drop dead
My wordiness, my sounding out my name, Larry, scares
                                                everything away,
As if I or my other truer self existed.

"Let Progress Pass You By"

—The Delphic Oracle

Life is a pigeon high transformed into a macaw
If you allow yourself to go asleep in the backyard
And let progress pass you by on its infinitely destructive course.
"Slow down, think small" they used to say in print
And now someone has whispered this to you in a backdoor john
You come up to the front of the house and cast your votes for
being late
A thousand things jump at you all demanding to be done
I will tackle them one by one and never get to the end, end
Listen to what the Delphic Oracle has for you, You pay as you
enter
If you do not believe the words she says through smoke and fuzz
From the tripod of her fire, "You've got to cut down on your
numbers
Stop playing Vegas with population—no more gets to populate
The nest we chickens made, maybe one or two, but open arms are
a bore
When they're millions wanting more, be nice but never advertise,
never, never advertise."

Las Huertas

What happened to the Gardens? We used to have one
We let it all go to weeds, we used to have a lot of stuff.
Too much trouble. Too much time. It didn't fit the romantic
        picture
Growing your own food, too complicated, in short
Too much work for too little reward. True
It tasted great—those tomatoes, etc. etc. etc. etc.
But, now is the time for all good people
To come to the band-aid of their country, and that's the gross
National product, not spending so much time without a paycheck
To show you your work was worth it. Not spending time with
The plants, the plants, not the infinite worry over bugs
And how to kill them, avoid them, prevent them, grow
The plants into their glory, not the peace of mind that comes
        from rewarding ground,
And living only, only where there's water & hope these crops are
        our organic future.

Rivaling

Angels and Visitations. Oh Rival Poet
Why are you so successful, and I'm such a clod.
I guess I went off the course by courting you—
Thinking that success would easily come my way if
I worked hard & dogmatically, offering all my substance to
God, or Coatlicue. I have given everything to every
Item of my existence and I still give. I am the post-post-
Modern equivalent of a non-pigeon hole, I simply
Grow my gardens in order to exist, I mean, live.
But you, oh W.S., oh magician Merlin
Oh Voice of the past, telling me what to do—
Ancient Greeks that are forever young, oh young—
Oh sex of literature guide me, I am no older than
The beauty you become, the beautiful, I'm sorry, my species is
Mutating in me, in you young lovely rival, I mean, what poetry
becomes.

Sword of Love

When Love tempers and doesn't get harder
It's so romantic, it flies off the handle
And I can catch you almost when I want you
Almost all the time is when I get you.
That is an embrace and we touch the face
That is a kiss and a hug   and a kiss.
That is strongest love that older and more easy
As the time of day when everything is pleasing.
That, my dear, is rare. There is a time of day when we
Can be free to hold on to life as if it isn't passing
Bye-bye! I've got you. It's a sword made of three
Kinds of metals beaten into swirling shape
And plunged sizzling into the water bath, that's
Home at last this love is no act.

Golden Shadows of the Flowers

Golden shadows of the flowers of love—
Is that what I'm always speaking of?
Or the yearning wish-I-had, wish-I-had, wish-I-had
In that way everybody is the same unless they lay themselves
To blame and pretend reality of life does not exist—
Yearning and, *or* love, usually both that play in the shadows
Where you and I walk, along the rustling water,
The irrigation flow and every time I return to the flower,
Say last night when this aromatic large spidery bloom opened up
For us all to admire as if we were tropical night insects,
And the last sun of sunset, catches on the walls
In the same shadows of leaves once and for all
    This voice, minute, of mine, that only says it lingers on
    Into the best time of day, tonight, this morning, it's gone.

When a Poet

for Paul Blackburn

He was a poet when a poet could be a poet
Not a dandy when a dandy is just another dandy.
I got the news and the news was not good but the news
Is never good when you get the news.
You were the only one who befriended my wife
she was pregnant, quiet and all the writers stood up
For other things. You were you, Paul we met the first
And last time in that Berkeley San Francisco Mills College light.
Standing on porches, drinking down silences
While they were arguing, the snobs against the pompous
The intellectual weight of the evangelical fringe
The gospels of poetry were meshed against each other.
You stood the way, the glasses, the palms behind the moustache
You smoked, and wrote. You become and are more than a poet.

Duo

for Marcia Latham

Fog over the fog, as everywhere I walked, there was a road under
      where I walked.
And the rain lasted all night on the snow, till there was mud.
One year touched lips with another year, and the hill disappeared
      into the sky of itself—
Great cycles became circles, circles of circles in the white light of
      Winter,
And the tops of the house were wet, just like the bottom.
The Christmas lights glowed & bubbled on the lintel over the
      kitchen window,
And I saw through the reflection of myself everything
Repeated, completed, and barely begun before it's over.
Heating leftovers as the fog comes through the window
And the leftover apples, frozen, now thawed, hang on the apple
      trees still, like decorations.
A month of lunches begins again when you don't know when
      you'll die, but will.
The living seems bent on killing, but you produce decent care for
      others and don't even own a weapon.
The colors keep you going, more intense than even if you were blind,
And the seeds, like ladies in waiting, in the ground, below the
      turkeys, in the packages, & in catalogs of efflorescences.

Renew

The body responds by opening flowers of fine titties.
Hand over the archaic become new & renewed.
To 'fess up. Honesty purifies, again & again & again.
I luh, I luh, lo, I get up in the middle of the night,
3 o'clock, fish tank bubbling, I luh, luh, lo
lore. I love yaw, I lub yore, willing open touched,
unlike the fish in there—vertical, still, the beautiful discus,
                    worm-eater
hardly moving, fish sleep, eyes open, you can't touch but look
unlike the fish, you Pisces opening flower covered inner, outer, open
woman, I touch lying towards human sleep awaiting
reading, touching holding, in the paradise of September moved
                    onto October
the month of opening lub, loof, love from exhausting harvest
& the waiting game for frost to come holding out plump
                    tomatoes.
In this extended sentence of life, freed at last to be who we are,
                    love renews.

Ears Please Too

(Self portrait to make me feel good)

Larry Goodell is a poet whose overdose on poetry
Has left him inebriated for life, like the Zen student
Whose shins have been kicked by the Zen master.
He tries to keep from falling asleep at the wheel,
Staying alert to the seasons, the means for any
    Reasons for the personification of life, botanicals
Leading mere man & woman, mere scent of poetry
As stars fold over, collide & expand
And the great rough mystery is constantly pacified.
He's definitely on the side of the rightful conquered
Godflying his way back through insect friends
To some accomplishment, though low profile, to honor spring
Now as the beginning of a dizzying voice:
Does he hear you, does he hear, alive, alert & aware?

Boogie on the Square

The light that is the fair, the light that is the fair
We boogie on the square, we boogie on the square
And know no one is soon, and know no one is soon
And know no one is far, as far as Zanzibar
But here and now and nimble, quick & ordinary
Depending on how you look at anything, if you look
If you look like a canary or
If you look like yourself, or
If you look *and* don't look, like
Anything or anyone or any look looks like—
Boogie on the square & move everywhere
Be little and big, customary and aware
The light is fair and travels in and out and
Picks up the board like a carpet anywhere, an-y-where.

All of Love

I can have all of love, played to a tired cello
Perked up to Bach's best, the message drums in the Congo
the cello, the Congo, the amazing Amazon, the woman
the River, the unpolluted Ocean, the nature harmonizers
the voices of the Globe in multivarious harmonies.
Two hundred & fifty years ago the music is still young
Buoyant to any mood, unaccompanied cello accompanied
in this life by this life I mean, a flower in the atmosphere
one gives the other to imagination. Three moonflowers the other
                                            night
and the orchid cactus from the canopies of Guatemala
blooming one two three blooms on successive nights
in full burst of exotic white, sweetness and strange,
to wilt in the morning, we sleep in the only sleep there is side
by side by and in the aromatic air with rain, the late summer gone.

The House That Makes It So

for the Creeleys

I drove by the old Creeley house
      because I wanted to write a poem.
There was the piano-shaped bedroom
      Bobbie had Von Shutze build.
The floors of adobe with sheep's blood sealer
      that kept crumbling in the old house,
The step-down new studio with that volcanic Jemez view
      where we sat & picked the energy of language apart
and I could put my life in art back together
      to go on in this isolated New Mexico way
where the others all seem taller, and I
      sit & improvise only sometimes to connect.
Their talking out the window of VW rebuilt engines
      or collaborations with Rauschenberg or Altoon,
The patio of corn & rhubarb & music to enchiladas
      Almaden white wine as
Back to the kitchen, the slow night weaved on
      and alternative worlds to where I was born
Played over the cassette player or hi-fi out to space
      and Max, or John, I never saw, or

Stan & Jane & Ed & Tuli & Jonathan & Ronald & Ann & George
     & on & on came through (I forgot Allen & Lawrence),
To meet like Gertrude Stein's patio in their adobe hacienda
     where children pulled apart & adults prospered
and friends analyzed until the dawn trailed off
     the always fresh love of poetry that was life, life blood.
If apprenticeship is anything, or hand to hand, a better poem
     commands itself to be written in the house that makes it

          so.

Down the Road of Life

(parental advice)

Cross your P's & toss your I's   open up your dusty doors
Dust, dust, dust   until there is no floor
Be on time on a dime   polish up your Q's
Be the Muse   & tell yourself what to do.

Put on your jacket   before going out late.
Come back from your date   before the cock crows.
Do as you wish   just like your pet fish,
Swimming waiting till the time you feed them from above.
Keep washed & don't stink, & set up a goal.
It doesn't sound so crazy if you have to have a mink stole
But do go to the ends of earth to help the starving populace
And remember trees like the giant sequoia or bristlecone pine,
Pacing out the time when you come to your senses
And what is most near becomes most dear & avoid
                    the avenues of fear.

Footnotes

for Lenore

All art passed before me in the form of plants
All the rules and regulations of the sport stopped,
As we, the only biology with botany in the lead
Rebuild or allow to rebuild, the ABC's
Of the Tao, the voices from the Aspens, where their leaves
Dropped almost instantly this Fall, as if they forgot to turn—
Humus anything you add to make it better, makes it better—
Completes the circle, breathing in, the plants that are remaking
The Earth, the dirt if you can find clean dirt,
Good, clean, dirt, enrichening the soil
Is a matter of transportation the plants' way of doing it
Is rising and falling, green crop manure,
Into the organic matter, possessing the Gods of the earth
The manlets, the womanlets, let's see, what's right at my feet.

COLOPHON

Set in CENTAUR,
designed by Bruce Rogers in «1912-14».
Though classic Venetian in homage,
its serif edges form an elegant offbeat,
like stride-piano riff-run plunks.
The look of words given music.
Frederic Warde cut a version of *Arrighi*
in «1929» for Monotype to accompany
as a chancery-style italic.

•

Book design by J. Bryan

Larry Goodell was born in Roswell, New Mexico—
where crossing cattle trails meet the Pecos River
and outer space visitors. He lives with his family
on the northern edge of the Sandia Mountains
in Placitas Village.